FUNDRAISING

10 Tips to Raise Money for NGOs, Small Business and Non-Profits (Including Startup and Nonprofit Fundraising Ideas, Strategies and Techniques for Entrepreneurs)

By MORGAN METZ

Table of Contents

Before You Start

You should get essential funds for your startup or NGO, but it is not an easy job. It is really difficult to perform different operations without money. Fundraising is a challenge in any economic climate, but it is important to use effective tools and strategies to get money for your business. Every organization typically needs income to manage different activities, pay different expenses, and pay the wages of labors and numerous other things.

You may get numerous donors, but they will not be ready to pay you for your business. It is essential to understand their psychology and work to understand their requirements. You have to write a business proposal because this will help you to persuade your reader. It should be written in a friendly tone and get long-term advantages. This book is designed for your help so that you can create a suitable plan and proposal. Your donor base will play an important role in the success of your business.

You should focus on the future and plan short term and long term benefits. It is important to understand the strategies and tools of fundraising. These will help you to get the advantage in the long-run. You should understand the needs of fundraisers and write a plan to impress them. Read this book because it will help you to write a plan and proposal. This will be a great chance for you to understand the needs of your donors.

Chapter 1: Introduction

In this challenging economy, it is really difficult for most of the nonprofit organizations and small businesses. Money is essential to perform different operations of a business and NGO and fundraising is a right way to get money for your business. Fundraising is a challenge in any economic climate, but it is important to use effective tools and strategies to get money for your business. Every organization typically needs income to manage different activities, pay different expenses, and pay the wages of labors and numerous other things. You should have a reliable fundraising plan to persuade fundraisers to offer you money.

Without fundraising, no strategy and plan will work effectively for the success of your business. Your fundraising strategies will help you to reduce financial risk and increase your profit. Money is always required for the development and expansion of your business. It is important to do more work for your existence and profitability. You can grow your business with the help of successful fundraising. You should get more than one donor so that you can reduce dependence only on one donor. It is important to always have an alternative and for this purpose, you should broad your fundraising to reduce dependency.

It is not easy to get money from a donor because they always want powerful reasons to give money. Your organization requires a volume of supporters and everyone is important for you. They will help you to create a sustainable organization. Your donor base will play an important role in the success of your business. You should focus on the future and plan short term and long term benefits. It is important to understand the strategies and tools of fundraising. These will help you to get the advantage in the long-run.

This book is designed for your help so that you can understand the methods and strategies of fundraising. This book has sure-fire techniques that will help you to get money for your business organization and NGO.

Chapter 2: Fundraising Tools for NGOs and Small Businesses

There are a few fundraising tools that are simple to use and proves helpful to get money for both NGO and small business organizations.

Design a Website

In the first step, you should design your own website to ensure your online presence. It is best to design a mobile-optimized website based on CMS (Content Management System) to make a good first impression. It will be impressive to update your website on a regular basis to share great details with your customers. You should update your activities for the information of your donor and give details of noble causes. You can get the advantage of different tools to design the websites of your NGO, such as Squarespace, Weebly, and Wix to launch modern websites with mobile compatibility. Website templates often include integration with social media and advertisements.

NGO can use WordPress for your website and download free or low-cost themes to design your website. Major traffic can be directed to your websites via mobile; therefore, you should design a mobile-optimized website. There is no need to hire a designer to design website because these free resources are enough for your guidance and help. If you are facing problem in the designing work, you can get the advantage of graphic students or volunteers to complete your work within your budget.

Launch a Newsletter

Newsletter or e-newsletter will be a great way to increase your chances to get online donations in developed countries. It will be good to publish your e-newsletter once or twice in a month and send via e-mail, iContact, MailChimp, and Constant Contact to make your launch simple. Some NGOs often use BCC to send e-newsletters and it is important to send a BCC to control spam and reduce the chances blockage by a server. Email communication is a good choice for you to distribute your newsletter. You can design an email list to send an e-newsletter and publish it on your website or blog. There should be a sidebar on your website or blog to promote your work.

Online Donations

For some small business organizations or NGOs, it will be difficult to accept online donations. Regulations for donations and online payments may vary in different organizations and you should check these regulations. If it is possible for you to accept online donations, you should manage an online account and accept online donations. You can get the advantage of PayPal and other methods to accept donations in 76 currencies. With the help of Ammado.com, it is possible to enable NGOS in various countries to accept donations.

You can adjust a "Donate Now" button on your home page and every page of your website and blog. You can create a separate "Donate" page to give details of online payments, mail funds, wire funds and mobile money. Your e-newsletter should also include "Donate Now" button and send urgent fundraising appeals to your e-newsletter.

Mimic Other NGOs and Organizations

Small NGOs can learn from other organizations and social media campaigns of successful NGOs. You can analyze their websites, donation pages and subscribe to their e-newsletters. You can get started with "Transparency International, UNICEF, Care International, Greenpeace International and Oxfam International". Similarly, it will be good to visit a website of the similar business organization to know about their fundraising efforts.

Facebook Page of NGO

You should create a Facebook page of your NGO to ensure your presence on social media. It will be good to tell the story of your NGO and offer status updates on social media. Try to explain your noble causes and activities to persuade donors to donate money. If it is difficult for you to set up your Facebook page, you can visit the Facebook pages of a few successful NGOs and business organizations. It will be good to write your fundraising strategy for your nonprofit organization.

Chapter 3: Fundraising Strategies and Plans for NGOs and Small Business

A small NGO or business organization often requires a successful source of income. You can write a grant proposal to increase funding. There are numerous ways to generate nonprofit funding, such as:

Events

Fundraising can be easy with the help of different events and these are common in the nonprofit world. You can get the advantage of events easily find in a weekly newspaper and you will find a number of local events put by nonprofit organizations. Events will engage your constituents and let people help you by supporting your organization in almost every event. There are different kinds of events that are often organized by nonprofit organizations:

- There will be an event to run and walk where the participants can pay a particular amount of money to participate. It will encourage others to come and donate, such as family, friends, and colleagues.

- You can organize dinners for live conferences, auction, and other activities get money from this event.
- The online auction is also useful to get money.
- Holiday themed events can be organized, such as Santa events, haunted house, valentine events, fall festivals and chocolate-related activities.
- Casino trips, tours, and other events will be great for publicity and earn money.

Earn Income

You can earn income by offering services and the revenue from goods and services will be good for your organization. If you have physical space, you can establish a museum and small stores, sell gift items, auction, etc.

Keep track of your earned money for goods and services. There are lots of rules about the income of charitable and nonprofit organizations and you should consider these rules.

Annual Appeal

A nonprofit organization is constructed for a noble cause and you should promote your causes to get funds. You can make an annual fundraising appeal to increase the possibility of fundraising. You can send an appeal via direct-mail in late fall or during holidays because people will feel more generous and look ahead to donate to reduce taxes. It will be good to get the advantage of the annual event to make an appeal for fundraising.

Membership

If membership of your organization makes sense, you can offer membership on the monthly and annual basis. It will help you to get income on a monthly basis and annual basis. It will be a great mean to get income and send renewal notices to your members. You can get a good source of income to handle the activities and causes of your organization.

Capital Campaign

A capital campaign will help you to generate donations for specific causes and activities. You can replace old programs with a new one because the campaigns are for a finite period of time. These are designed to collect a targeted sum of money. The campaigns can be helpful to manage your monetary goals and receive money via silent phase. If you want monetary benefits, you should announce your campaign to public by increase the confidence of donors that your campaign is successful.

Tips to Design a Fundraising Strategy

A fundraising strategy can be helpful for you to increase funding for your NGO and small business organizations. There are a number of ways to design appropriate fundraising strategy:

Design a Case to Get Support

A powerful argument should explain the reasons and problems to give a valid reason for the donation. It should explain:

- Actual problem
- Possible solution for this problem
- Benefits of donations and differences in case of success
- Consequences of failure
- Qualification of your organization to tackle different problems.

It is important to explain it in a simple and focused manner by keeping the tone emotional and engaging.

Analysis and Plan

In this step, you will decide the focus on a mixed portfolio so that you shouldn't depend on a single source. Every source has its particular importance and properties. You should plan to exploit these resources with a different timeframe. There are a few options:

Foundations and Trusts: You can get new organizations for funding or get a donation from existing organizations.

Companies: Business organizations often contribute in a variety of methods from cash to commodities and services. You should manage relationships in different forms in a win-win situation.

Local: In different communities, there is a wide range of organizations, such as schools, groups, and churches. You can raise money with their collaboration.

Individuals: You can get large or small personal contributions on a regular basis.

Structure

You should know the right sources to approach because it will help you to structure your fundraising in an appropriate manner. You should create a fundraising committee or outsource a consultant. If you want to increase funding in the long term, you should build your fundraising capacity.

Research

It is important to research your potential donor, understand his psychology and design a plan for successful fundraising. You should search potential people and organizations that can easily support you and meet your different needs. It is important to start with close contacts, senior staff, and other people for help to reach potential people to donate.

You should write a proposal and ask for money. Foundations and trusts can help you to get a good amount of money. Try to give them a reason to donate and feel satisfied. If you have any existing donor, you should work hard to build strong relations.

Chapter 4: Tips to Write a Proposal for Fundraising

You have to write a proposal to convince your donor for the solution of problems that you want to address and important resources for smooth functioning. You should write a proposal to convey your needs to potential donor, such as:

Unsolicited Proposal

You should write an unsolicited proposal at any time or according to a particular date to meet with the particular panel.

Response to Specific Program

It is important to give a response to a specific donor agency and you should follow a guideline issued by this agency to write your proposal. These programs have particular deadlines and you should follow these deadlines.

Response to Call for Proposals (RFP)

You should respond to an RFP to write a proposal for the support of your project. It should fit your specific needs and design a work statement for the funding agency. It may have a particular deadline and you should consider these deadlines.

Response to Tender

You can send a response to tender advertisements available in local newspapers and these instructions should be followed completely.

After writing a proposal, it may take a while to obtain required funds. Even a perfectly designed proposal submitted according to the guidelines can be rejected.

Important Rules to Write a Proposal

There are a few important rules that should be followed while writing a proposal. It will help you to increase the accuracy and success chances:

It Should be Concise

Every proposal is written as per its particular guidelines, but a rule of thumb is to keep it brief and comprehensive. It should not exceed more than 4 to 5 pages and keep yourself in the shoes of the donor. They will not like page after page because they don't have time to read this. Your proposal should be interesting enough to grab the attention of potential donors. A concise proposal can highlight your request to get money for a particular cause.

Positive and Passionate

You should write a proposal in a confident and positive tone. Keep it in mind that you are going to sell a concept and it should have a positive impact on the mind of the reader. It is important to avoid the use of conditional language, such as I would like, we can include, possible outcomes will be, etc. It will be good to use a bold and confident tone, such as results will be, the event will include and we will, etc.

Write a Unique Proposal for Every Funder

Every funder will have his/her own packages, financial strategies, policies, and financial plans. You should focus on these guidelines to make your application contextualized. Funders may ask questions, call you or help you, but you have to do your homework. Your proposal should present vision, planning, and research. It is important to search important details and include relevant information to make a solicited request.

Your funder may provide a format and you should follow this format carefully. A successful proposal should target the needs of organizations. Careful planning and research can make it successful. There is no need to use jargon and keep it simple and clear. Write almost 20 percent problems related to the grant. There are a few factors that are really important for a funder:

- Feasibility
- Purpose of project
- Importance of project for community
- Accountability of applicant
- Competence to successfully manage a project.

Important Section of a Proposal

- Title page containing name of organization for funding, contact details and important names
- Table of content to write the list of important sections of proposal with page numbers
- Abstract to highlight the main content of the proposal
- Needs statement or problem statement to include problems of your business

- Goals and objectives of your proposal to identify expected outcomes
- Project plan to write important steps to execute the project
- Evaluation of project results and explain the project plans
- Write the name of key personnel and give a brief description of qualifications and responsibilities
- Equipment and facilities that will be used in the project
- Project budget, salaries of personnel and material cost
- Appendices and curriculum vitae of the main personnel will be an important part of the proposal.

You should write a proposal according to the given guidelines to increase success chances of your proposal.

Chapter 5: Skills to Influence Funder for Donation

There are a few skills that will help you to impress your funder to give you a donation. These skills will prove really helpful:

Organizational Skills

It is the most important skill of successful people to handle their responsibilities. They are trustworthy people and make sure to complete their every work on time. With the help of their organizational skills, they can prioritize important tasks and find reliable solutions to every problem.

Communication Skills

Strong communication is an essential element of success because you need to communicate in a better way to share details with clients and co-workers. You should be a good communicator and an active listener. You can use different methods, such as email, Skype, Phone, social media and face-to-face meetings.

Negotiation Skills

The confident and influential nature is required to become a good negotiator. The negotiating skills are required in personal and professional lives to make your regular life beneficial and pleasant. Your negotiation skills may help you get a pay raise, promotion, and new clients.

Emotional Intelligence

To become a successful person, you should be able to understand and relate to others with the help of your emotional intelligence. Emotional intelligence can help successful people to deal effectively with their clients and co-workers. You should put yourself in the shoes of other people to increase your emotional intelligence.

Critical Thinking

It is a useful skill for successful people solve problems and detect errors in a system in a creative manner. A critical thinker can solve problems after accessing the situation quickly.

Focused and Objective

Successful people often have their focus on long-term objectives and dreams. You should be able to focus on your future and track regular problems to increase your success chances. You should have the ability to find out focal point and problematic areas to work on them.

Balance Skills and Personality

Balance plays an important role in the lives of successful people because they always have a healthy foundation. You should be able to organize tasks efficiently without increasing stress and increase the possibilities of success. With the help of balance, you can manage your personal and professional life in a better way, without mingling them.

Teamwork

If you are writing a proposal for a project, you should express your teamwork skills. Teamwork is a most important skill required to complete the job successfully. You may work on a project with your boss and teammates. They will work with a partner and you should learn to respect the point-of-view of all people in your team. If you are lacking team skills, it will slow down the success and progress rate of each project.

Confidence and Trust

You should show your trust and confidence because the funder likes to select reliable people. The successful people can't trust time, but they have full faith in their development skills. They work with confidence for their own benefits. If you want to improve your confidence, you should work on your body language and social skills. Try to be polite and respect others to earn respect in response.

Research and Analytical Skills

It is the most important skill of successful people. You should have an ability to research required information and analyze it as per your needs. It is important to become proactive and respond quickly after analyzing a situation or a given set of data. It will help you to improve the current situation. You should research about your funder and carefully analyze his/her mood while talking. It will help you to get positive results in funding.

Chapter 6: Design a Business Plan for Funder

If you want fundraising for your small business, it is important to start a successful business plan. There are a few tips to design a successful business plan:

Successful Business Model

You need to have a successful business model to stand out in the crowd. A particular shop can be successful for many reasons, and you need to survey the common elements as well as the rare qualities. After the completion of your market research, you need to develop an idea to make your small business successful. It doesn't mean to follow the business plan of another store, but you should have your own business plan. You need to consider your online store just like a physical business and lay a strong foundation for your business. To increase your success chances, you should consider the following elements:

- Design and layout of your shop
- Accessibility and easy navigation
- Color schemes and fonts
- Range of products and number of listings

- Price, description of the products, photographs, materials and the keywords
- Packaging and shipping
- Branding and networking
- Business cards, signature designs and marketing campaigns
- Communication of the niche and other organizations.

Importance of a Unique Business Plan

The basic purpose is to consider all the qualities that you found in various shops during your research and put them all together. This will help you to create a good business plan, but it is important to give your own unique touch to the business plan. There is no need to reinvent everything, but research is always essentials. There are lots of examples where the business organizations take a start from scratch without spending most of the time in research. Its final outcomes were a failure or lower profitability. The advance research will help you to make your work easy and increase your chances of success as well.

Your business plan should be based on the particular needs of the market, and for this purpose, you should get the opinion of your customers. Identify your target audience and know their needs to offer similar products to make them happy and satisfied. It will be good to conduct an online market survey to have a better idea about the expectations of the customers. Find out the weaknesses of your competitors and remove all these problems from your products to offer something special in the market. Let your customer know that you value their needs and opinions.

The internet makes it really easy to make money because you can turn your hobby into a business. You can start your own business with short and long-term goals. There are hundreds of internet sellers who are able to use their skills to start their own business. The best thing is a convenience because you can start your own shop without previous business and marketing experience. It is really simple for anyone to have a start. Your hobby will help you to generate a profit because the people like to buy unique and hand-made products. Since it is easy to start a business, but it is important to differentiate yourself from others. You may face a tough competition to understand the requirements of the target audience.

There can be lots of other shops offering similar products and services, but you should know the ways to highlight your products by explaining how these are unique. You have to establish your own brand name to increase the profitability of your business. This book is particularly designed for you because the step-by-step guidance will help you to understand the requirements of an online shop. The book contains 30 marketing strategies that can increase your profit. Keep it in mind that without proper marketing, you will not be able to spread your business.

Promote Your Business in a Better Way

There are lots of ways to grab the attention of people to your services, and you should know the exact way that will work for your business. From the beginning to end, you are going to learn the ways to become a first-rate entrepreneur. The book has basics of setting up your shop for the beginners, and the marketing strategies to increase the visibility of your business. You will come to know the use of social media tactics to increase the traffic of your Internet shop.

In short, the Internet is a household name, and you can learn the top ways to make money in your own way. It will make the road of success easy for you because you can learn the ways to grab the attention of the target audience. This book will serve as a roadmap for you because it is written in a simple and friendly manner. You should make a business plan and share it with a potential donor to get funding for your business.

Chapter 7: Common Mistakes to Avoid in Fundraising

Fundraising is really important for NGOs and small business organizations; therefore, you should avoid a few mistakes that can ruin your plan:

Wrong Amount of Money

This is a major problem that can be a hurdle in your fundraising objectives. You should collect important details about potential funder and find out his/her potential before asking for a particular amount. You may ask more or less because of lack of research.

Lack of Thankful Attitude

If you are working with an old funder, it is important to maintain long-term relations on good terms. You should write a thank you letter on every support to acknowledge their efforts. Some people make a mistake and unable to say thanks for getting funds. It can irritate your funder and he/she may not be happy with your attitude.

Lack of Personal Calls and Visits

You should stay in touch with donors because 94 percent donors complain that nonprofit organizations completely ignore them after taking support. You should cultivate good relations and make them feel special and important. A personal call and thank you will be a good move for you.

Special Events Can be Difficult to Raise Money

People often organize special events to raise money without realizing the difficulties in their way. You should understand that these things can be difficult and it is important to work properly with planning to avoid all mistakes. You should grab the attention of people and there are lots of ways to grab the attention of people to your services, and you should know the exact way that will work for your business. From the beginning to end, you are going to learn the ways to become a first-rate entrepreneur. The book has basics of setting up your shop for the beginners, and the marketing strategies to increase the visibility of your business. You will come to know the use of social media tactics to increase the traffic of your Internet shop.

Focus on the company of knowledgeable people and read more books. The books, magazines, articles, and journals can increase your knowledge, motivation and inspiration. It is a nutritious food for your mind because the books will enlighten your mind with a new light and you can use this light to generate new ideas and drive your mind on a positive road.

Try to select knowledgeable material, such as books, periodicals, and articles. The negative material will increase your negativity and you may find yourself on the path of crime. Keep it in mind that action and fighting fiction and movies can increase emotions of violence and these are not fruitful for you. Relevant education and training can increase your confidence and you can speak confidently in public without any fear.

Conclusion

Without fundraising, no strategy and plan will work effectively for the success of your business. Your fundraising strategies will help you to reduce financial risk and increase your profit. Money is always required for the development and expansion of your business. It is important to do more work for your existence and profitability. You can grow your business with the help of successful fundraising. You should get more than one donor so that you can reduce dependence only on one donor. It is important to always have an alternative and for this purpose, you should broad your fundraising to reduce dependency on one party.

Money and wealth are two important parameters of success, but it is important to understand the right aspects of success. For some people, achievement, freedom and ability to accomplish different tasks are important elements of success. If you want to become a successful person, you should have some special traits. These traits can help you to achieve your goals. You should understand the basic needs of a project before taking a final decision. It is important to select a right donor to finance your projects and start working with knowledgeable people.

Passion is really important for you to accomplish something in your life. If you love what you are doing, it will help you to develop other important success traits. There are two types of people, seekers, and strivers. You should increase your traits to get the advantage of available resources.